Disclaimer

Also by Tim Chipps

Make America Right Again

Ominous Alliance

Gross Injustice

Citizens Handbook

National Preservation
or
National Perversion

Published and distributed by
Artisan Vintage Works

Printed in the United States of America

To order this publication
please visit our website:
www.artisanvintageworks.com

ATTENTION!

••• NEWS – ALERT •••

The following is a *Snooze Presentation* brought to you
by *Flake News*.

CeNdeNd The Compromised Networth of 0.
Guaranteed to be Spun.

By *Spinister* - the Twisted News Source

"Common-Daters"
Host: *Pandersome Grouper* – ("A Guy's Guy!")
and
Hostess: *Ratesfell – Matics* – ("A Gal's Gal!")

All of the pre-fabricated, nonsensical fables told in this series are the sole opinion of this networth. *CeNdeNd* and it's
affiliates are not responsible, and remain fully unaccountable
for it's contempt, and reserve the right to be radically dis-
torted, dishonest, and un-American in presenting the satire
commentary featured as

"Clueless in Politics – Follyhood."

<u>WARNING</u>
CONTAINS CENSORED MATERIAL:
If you are a liberal and cannot perceive reality,
You should definitely read this!

Introduction

Our story begins back in the fall of 2015. It was during the presidential campaign. I began to notice many commercials and news clips with our old friends from Hollywood voicing their opinions in strong opposition to the republican candidate Donald J. Trump.

I figured it was just another Hollywood political rally expressing their far left liberal views and dismissed it at that. It did not take long to realize that a *tenacious* and *ravenous* onslaught of attack was being levied against Mr. Trump especially, targeting his character and stability as an individual. I realized that this was an orchestrated and intentional effort on behalf of the extremely biased liberal media *minions* and the "Democratic party" to de-legitimize Republican candidate Trump in an all out effort of *voracity.*

What is so ironic about these old and mostly-retired Hollywood elites is the profound hypocrisy each one of them displayed in their tireless effort to characterize a successful businessman who worked his tail off for 70 years while these bimbletons in *Follyhood* live their soap opera bubble existence, pretending to be members of our society here in the U.S.A. So I compiled much of this nonsense into a skit for your enjoyment and entertainment. After all, that's what show biz is all about!

I hope you can enjoy this satire on *Follyhood.*

It all started in *Clevorly Stills*,
in the sunny, funny *city of Follyhood*...

Now, Robber He's NoHero came and stole a part from *Pew Heffer*, in the Don Juan - debunked series: "Barrel of Despicables" featuring *Shrillary Sinton* and *Hairy Steed*. Not long after this failed, *Robber* would soon find his part, striving as a low life punk underworld mobster, wandering on a day-by-day basis, searching for a meaningful life. That's when he met *Barbee Strife Land*. *Barbee* considered herself to be quite influential and she intended to make a real big impression on *Shrillary*.

Now *Barbee* was considered a mysterious mistress to *Robber,* who was rather loathsome. The fact is *Barbee* was mistress of many, but she was particularly fond of *Robber.* That's where *Robber* broke in. He saw an opportunity to steal a part from *Barbee*, so he did. But he got nailed and called *Spill Sinton* for advice about how to lie when you get caught in the act.

Spill Sinton was the husband of *Shrillary* and an expert in the art of deceit. He even fooled *Shrillary* about his life-long obsession as a pedimonger. What's worse, she retrieved him time and time again from the cesspool of debauchery he stayed so entrenched in. She did this even when *Spill* was pretending to be a leader and got caught in his dark room engaging in his unmentionable misbehavior. *Spill* was finally disbarred and impeached for his countless misdeeds, but this did not stop *Shrillary*! She boldly denied any of *Spill's* gross and vile misconduct and even claimed it was a vast right wing theory of conspiracy to frame her estranged husband.

She went on to be an unsuccessful Senatorium and then, under the Nomadic Admistray-shun, she was woefully and with grim expectations, appointed as the Secularly of State. This did not go well. She had all of America's top secrets hacked, then spent her restless time trying to keep tabs on *Spill*, while giving favors away in billions to foreign governments and pocketing the rest of America's hard-earned tax dollars through the *Spill* and *Shrillary Sinton Frowndation*. What a stinking mess! Then she went running from her office, pretending she would be a good leader. Well, you know the rest of the story. At least she got rich from the bribery and she still had *Spill*–when she could find him.

In the meantime, back in *Follyhood*, *Barbee Strife Land* and *Robber He's NoHero* disgusted marriage. She said "I could never take your name, how would it sound? *Barbee He's NoHero*. Not a chance. Besides that, we can just remain fully uncommitted to anything real, and pretend we care." After all, I must remain the mysterious mistress if ever I have any hope of saving my name. She had quite the reputation to uphold and *Shrillary* needed all the handouts she could get.

Remember *Hairy Steed*? He was very jealous of others getting so much attention. So he decided to make a name for himself and reverted back to his childhood days as *Fuzzy Foal* (a baby stud). He celebrated by retiring after years and years of unproductive duties as a Senatorium, pretending to be a leader while accomplishing virtually nothing worthwhile."

Since we're back on the subject of politics, I mention *Schmuck Rumor* and *Nannie Poloosly*. Rumor has it that both will soon retire. After a long, gruesome career of tearing down America's values and blocking all positive initiatives, they will finally step down off the high horse of *Hairy Steed* and become just a bad memory in American politics. Besides, *Nannie* is under investigation for fraud and *Schmuck* is considering going down with the ship, so he decided to be the *Senatorium Minority Looser* and give it one more shot. (I guess we'll see in 2018.)

Meanwhile, back in *Follyhood*, a new guy appeared, *Gorge SoarNose*. Acting as a bouncer in the "Pay to Play" nonsense scheme show, *Gorge SoarNose* is one of the most infamous players that ever showed up. He, being a spoiled-rotten rich brat, inherited all his stealth, never having to work a day in his life and proud of it. His foreplay is financing bums and thugs everywhere. If you are a low life looking to get something for nothing, you need to see *Gorge SoarNose*. His sponsorship of illegal thug activities knows no boundary.

If you want to disrupt, vilify or start a riot, just call *Gorge*. He employs the irrelevant *All Sharpen* to cause insidious mob-like, terroristic activities and gatherings, with looting and mobs embarking in riots while chanting death threats to "officers of the peace." There is no limit to their malice in their intent to destroy, deface and demolish private and public property. The thugs and bums employed by *SoarNose* will attack and assault innocent victims who stand for a noble cause. These deadbeats led by the irrelevant *All Sharpen* are brutally disrespectful and unlawful as they wildly engage in pillaging, burning and destruction of everything in their path. It's surprising they are not in jail as instigators of riotous misbehavior and uncivil domestic terrorism. There is no amendment anywhere that permits this lawlessness.

I guess you could call *Errand Hold-On* to rescue you from trouble in an uncivilized case titled "Looser Life on the Streets" vs. "American Dignity." *MightCall Morgue* is a really big fan of old *Gorge SoarNose*. His failed attempts as a *Follyhood* non-producer brought him so low he could hardly get up off the couch. He and his close friend, *Dine On Fineswine*, care nothing at all about America's future. We all know they are the bad actors and instigators of civil unrest, yet shamelessly together they seek America's demise.

Don't forget the party poopers in *Follyhood*. Did I mention the *Poo-Party* that *Gords Looney* threw last week? All his favorites showed up. First *Wily Sighless* under-performed in a debunked song she wrote, *"Let's All Live on Broke Back Together."* *Melon DeGenerate* sang back up. *Hoodie Iceburg* and *Chair Solo* met in the spot tub with *Rougie No Model*, What a splash! Meanwhile, *As She Crud* came crawling up out of the abyss looking for *Madumba!* There in the background, *Rich-N-Smear* and *Pet Fiddler* spoke of doing a gig together. Lately *Ca Ca* called *Madumba* in a phony call, asking her to come over and join the *Squatting*.

You know the *Fun Bun Star Musty Show Flakes* can never get enough! After midnight the *Clevorly Stills* police were called to bring order to the crowd, but *Rougie No Model* stood up and demanded her right to be disorderly, disruptive and down right disgusting, as she always is. *Gords Looney* was issued a sightation and he promiscuously went back into his home. No further action was taken because they all passed out for the next 48 hours.

Did I tell you about the ill-fated trio? These notionless wonder women all escaped from the local nursing home. *Sully Feels, Shame Fond Of*, and *Merky Street* appearing in commercials featuring the attempted impediment of our new hard-working president. Don't forget to see the moaning *Merky Street*, in her *Olden Gloat Award, Retreat From Reality* speech. All covered by "The mass mediocre not worth a snooze organisms." Isn't it ironic, the satirical comedy of all the wanna bees working so hard to establish a colony of losers in *Follyhood's* pack! Hoo let the dogs in? Hoo? Hoo? Hoo? Hoo? *(It was Robber He's No Hero!)*

The *Follyhood Favs* are back at it. This time it's with a twist. *Mighty Mightcall Morgue* gave an innerlude with his shirt off. The film crew quit and the common-dater fled from the studio. The networth's owner had to pay for the innerlude set even though not a word was taped. It's not as if anything *Mightcall* would have said mattered anyway. *Armbro Sweatamonger* was featured in "The Apprentice" and he thought they said appendix, so he had his taken out. He signed up for English lessons and is wearing a sweat suit and adult briefs in case of an accident. He is not obsolete; he just insisted after his rhino behavior and turncoat comments that maybe his disposition could be redeemed, especially since allegations of colluding with the Russians surfaced.

The "Guys and Gals" parade will be smothered by *Ratesfell Matic. Rougie NoModel* will be brazen the way. *Pandersome Grouper* will be common-dater innerluding *Melon Degenerate.* Over at SMeL Networth *Skate McMinion,*

4

attempting to impersonate a woman of noble character, was likened unto a pig with a gold ring in her nose. *Smelisa McBarfie* and the snooze cruise team at CeNdeNd were very busy attempting to sling the contents of their potty chairs into the audience. Just another smelly day in *Follyhood*. All of the passion in the parade brought them back together though and they had a great big group hug publicly to prove it.

Skate McMinion and *Smelisa McBarfie* are both going through withdrawal and have been enrolled in rehabilitation programs. Suffering from ADDS (Attention Deficate Disorderly Syndrome), both are expecting little chance of rediscovering reality.

The fake news at Messy N'BCeded is snore-intoxicating and if that doesn't put you to sleep, watch *Pandersome Grouper* over at CeNdeNd. Everybody knows you can't get STRAIGHT talk from common-daters, especially from a "guy's guy" or a "gal's gal." Not in the city of pity, located in the armpit of *Smell-A*.

Follyhood is like never-never land. Nothing real ever happens there. It's simply a figmentation of anticipation. In other words, you will have to wait a long time to hear anything with adult content. Meanwhile, *Merky Street* appeared in the "Granny Awards," as ravaging as a bear without her cubs, spewing about delusions she has been having since the election of 2016. Her psychiatrist has placed her on heavy anti-hallucinogenic medication and very strong anti-depressants. This, combined with her sedatives, has really had a negative effect on her ability to function out in public or deal with reality. Her primary physician is hopeful of a full recovery, but insists it could take years and years of psychiatric counseling to regain her mental stability. We all hope she gets over it, real soon. The doctors would not comment any further on rumors of the diagnosis actually being HEDDS (Homenigmiatic Distress Disorder Syndrome). She did win the "Granny Award," even though the drama extravaganza wasn't impressive.

Meanwhile, in politics, Senatorium *Eliminate Warrants* (or *Pokehauntis)* was asked to sit down after numerous outbursts of unrestrained babbling followed by indistinguishable mutter and mumble sounds. This rarely occurs in the chamber of the U.S. Senate and experts agree it could be due to PHCS (Post-Homo Confinement Syndrome). After she was arrested in the Dakotas and jailed for unlawful criminal trespass and defacing private property, she submitted to a d.n.c. test and it was confirmed she is as white/albino as Gasper the Ghost. She had no further comments that were intelligible enough to distinguish in English, so she gave up the floor to *Dine on FineSwine*. After her squealing was done, *Nannie Paloosly* (Mouse Minority Leader) addressed the new president as George Bush! She had to be reminded he hasn't been the president for 30 years! She couldn't even remember last week. No need for concern there, just a touch of amnesia. After all, she is the minority leader in the Senate.

House minority speaker *Schmuck Rumor* was caught on screen pretending to cry. There appears to be an emotional breakdown in the d.n.c. *Spill Sinton* disappeared with the Energizer Bunny and *Shrillary* can't find him again. They've been singing "all my rowdy friends have settled down." Except *Gorge SoreNose*, he's being indicted for international scandals in the Balkans and in Europe. Good luck *Gorge*! See ya in Alcatraz!

If that's not enough to cause you hysteria, check out Watter's World on Saturdays on Fox News, doing interviews with college kids protesting and burning their schools down so they don't have to attend class. Can you imagine the class of 2016 running this country in a few years? It's really frightening. You better get your kids out of those colleges before the professors in those schools entirely brainwash your kids into Minions of Unemployment Socialist Elites or (M.O.U.S.E.). *Follyhood* is full of folks like that.

ATTENTION
NEWS ALERT

"Breaking Snooze"

It has been reported that **Maskqueen Wanders** and **All Rankin** both fell asleep during Senatorium proceedings review of Supreme Court justice appointment. When **Maskqueen Wanders** was suddenly startled awake, she began to insist that Russia invaded Korea last week and wondered what the new president was going to do. **All Rankin** was just released from the psychiatric ward for testing of his Cerebellum-Labotomistic-Infringementosis. Doctors and experts agree there is a very legitimate concern after half his brain was rendered dysfunctional. At his check-up **Nannie Paloosly** voiced her opinion as, quote, "**All Rankin** still has half a brain in his head, and that's all you need as a Democrat anyway!" What a great sigh of relief that came from reporters when **Nannie** announced the snooze clip on CeNdeNd.

Meanwhile, back in the Scrapital of California, **Ferry Crown**, the Coveter of the state, gave a speech, defending his disposition on allegations of his direct involvement in heisting 25 billion dollars of taxpayers' money and redistributing the money to illegal undocumented aliens he has been housing in his basement of the Coverter's mansion in Sacremendo. He stated firmly, quote, "I was elected by the fine citizens of California to do as I see fit with these state revenues, and I will continue in my unwaivering commitment to support, finance, house and protect all illegal aliens whom unlawfully enter the state of California." He continued, "I, **Ferry Crown**, am the Covetor of California and I have sworn an oath to protect, house, finance and support any foreigner who enters the state. Isn't this what you elected me to do?"

In an attempt to be "literally correct," the author will spell out virtually what the far left Flake News and Follyhood seem to have in common. There appears to be a consensus and similar theme among this group of people. They send a message to the American people day by day, and consistently it is the same.

What do they hope to ever accomplish? Champions of the lawless, they indulge in vain and conceited rhetoric regarding things they know nothing about.

The fabric these folks are made of comes from the same stock. What they all have in common is woven together with a thread, stitching a core pattern of behavior derived from the culture of pagan revelry, most believing we are beasts, having evolved from animals and holding to the far left, radical liberal, extremist ideology. This group displays very little tolerance for American traditional values and is quite outspoken on the issues pertaining to immorality. Their self-consuming vanity is the driving motivator and root cause of their condition.

If there was to be any hope for these people, it would require a radical uprooting from the very bad culture they have immersed themselves in. An excellent recommendation would be to disguise yourself as a real person, go out and work amongst real people for at least one year. At that point you could reassess your perspective of reality and possibly you could obtain the simulation of a real person and re-enter the human race with some idea of what is of importance and has value vs. what you are doing now that amounts to nothing. Wish you all the best.

See you in the next edition. That's all for now!

AMERICA'S MOST UNWANTED

Attention – Insurgent – Bulletin!

THE TOP 24 VIOLATORS

F	O	L	L	Y
H	O	O	D	
F	A	R		
L	E	F	T	
F	A	K	E	S

If you see any of these nobodies

WARNING! BE ALERT. DO NOT APPROACH THEM.

They all promised to leave America and lied.

REMAIN CALM. DO NOT ATTEMPT TO REASON.

The clues in their identity will be:

DENIAL ▪ ANXIETY ▪ FREQUENT FITS ▪ OUTBURSTS OF RAGE OR FEAR

They often have seizures, caused by Attention Deficit Disorder (ADD) Due to Homenigmiatic Tension Distress Syndrome (HTDS).

BE VIGILANT AND CONTACT US IMMEDIATELY: 1-WHO-ISIT?

Follyhood's
"Rap Sheet"
Song

You wouldn't refrain from being profane,
during the campaign.
No need to explain.
You got nothing to gain, now you're out in the rain.

Just carry your shame, don't blame it on fame.
You were lame in your game, now you got a bad name.
You remain to be vain, wow that is insane, look at the stain.

It causes you pain 'cuz you could not restrain
from your nasty disdain.
Now you cannot regain from the strain in your brain.

So just get on a train or maybe a plane.
Go to Ukraine or even to Spain.
You cannot maintain to stay in your lane,
it's like a ball and chain.

The truth is plain, you cannot sustain.
If you hope to remain you cannot falter again.
If you claim to be sane, you're going down the drain.

So you fain to retain your honor again as an American?
So just hang with the gang. Keep slinging your slang
while Old Liberty rang and freedom will reign
no matter what you proclaim.
You tried again and again but only in vane.

Reel News ©2017

www.ingramcontent.com/pod-product-compliance
Lightning Source LLC
Chambersburg PA
CBHW071345290326
41933CB00040B/2374